MW00945211

PROTECTING NURSING HOMES AND THEIR RESIDENTS
FROM THE
UNLICENSED PRACTICE
OF
LAW

JOHN R. FRAZIER,
LEONARD E. MONDSCHEIN
& TWYLA L. SKETCHLEY

ISBN: 978-1-4834-8174-6 (sc)
ISBN: 978-1-4834-8173-9 (e)

Lulu Publishing Services rev. date: 05/04/2018

CONTENTS

INTRODUCTION

As nursing home and assisted living facility managers and staff, you dedicate each day to assisting and protecting the seniors in your care. You also understand how families and elders can be bewildered by the admissions process and overwhelmed by their sudden financial situation.

This handbook raises awareness to an ethical and fiduciary tragedy that happens all too often to seniors throughout Florida. It occurs in nursing homes, assisted living facilities, retirement communities and any other settings where aging citizens reside.

> The tragedy is the **unlicensed practice of law**, commonly referred to as **UPL,** as it pertains to Medicaid planning.

Prepared by Florida Elder Law attorneys, this handbook serves to protect Florida long term care residents, and to also protect facility administrators and staff from engaging in or unintentionally supporting the unlicensed practice of law.

Together we find ourselves on the front line of elder care. In the chapters ahead, you will understand:

- what UPL is and how it happens,

- how to protect, prevent and deter nursing home and assisted living facility residents from becoming victims,
- how to protect yourself and your facility from becoming an unwitting participant to UPL activities, and
- important actions you can take to fight UPL if you see it happening.

CHAPTER 1

WHY YOU SHOULD USE AN ELDER LAW ATTORNEY FOR MEDICAID PLANNING

One of the biggest issues our seniors face is paying for long term care in a skilled nursing home or assisted living facility. Most seniors cannot afford up to $100,000 a year to live in a quality facility.

Florida's Medicaid program provides vital financial assistance to many seniors who need long term care.

Medicaid is a needs-based program. Besides *medical* eligibility requirements, the Medicaid program has strict *financial* guidelines that all applicants must meet. Many seniors exceed the financial limits – yet still cannot afford to pay the costs of the nursing home care they desperately need.

This is where the expertise of an elder law attorney who practices primarily in Medicaid law comes in.

Medicaid planning attorneys, also known as Elder Law attorneys, use the law to legally and ethically position Medicaid applicants within the income and asset guidelines for the Medicaid program. The attorneys are often able to preserve all or a portion of the senior's assets to support the senior's quality of life, without "spending down" all of their assets.

This is the basis of Medicaid Planning.

An attorney has a duty of loyalty only to their client and will do their best to achieve the client's goals. Proper handling of the legal aspects of Medicaid approval is critical to the senior's well-being, which includes prompt and proper payment for care.

A minefield of potential dangers for the unwary

Many seniors and their families are misled or deceived by people who promote themselves as "Medicaid Planners," but are not licensed attorneys.

They hold themselves out to be "experts" and "specialists" who can financially qualify the senior for nursing home Medicaid. But many may not have the senior's best interest in mind.[1]

The dangers that follow can be catastrophic for the senior. The consequences can also harm the facility in which the senior lives.

Often the aim of the nonlawyer "specialist" is to induce the senior into buying financial products.

Equally dangerous are people who have the best of intentions, and attempt to "help" seniors apply for and become eligible for Medicaid.

For example, some Florida nursing homes refer their patients to nonlawyer "Medicaid planning companies" to help them with the application process or with qualifying for benefits. This can lead to disastrous results.

These Medicaid planning companies are not always a senior's advocate. Their loyalties may lie with their own prosperity.

Incorrect advice, fraudulent planning activities or improperly prepared legal planning documents, from any nonlawyer source, can cause the senior to spend down their assets incorrectly, or transfer vital assets inappropriately—thus ruining the senior's chances to qualify for Medicaid.[2]

Eight reasons to use an elder law attorney (and NOT a nonlawyer) to assist in qualifying a person for Medicaid benefits:[3]

1. **Financial planners, insurance agents, etc. are making "hidden money"** on top of their service fee by selling "Medicaid Friendly" or "Medicaid Qualifying" annuities and related financial products. The planner or agent earns a commission from each sale. Worse yet, they don't have to disclose they are earning a commission – and thus are making hidden fees.[4]

2. **Annuity and insurance sales agents are by definition sales persons.**[5] Attorneys, on the other hand, have a *fiduciary* responsibility to their clients. (A person acting in a fiduciary capacity must act in the best interest of the client, and not in one's own best interest.)

3. **Nonlawyer Fees.** In addition to earning commissions, nonlawyer Medicaid planners typically charge a fee to prepare and submit applications to the Department of Children and Families.

4. **Nonlawyers are not licensed by the Florida Bar.**[6] There is no way to know if nonlawyers have training, knowledge or skills. To become an attorney one must have at least 7 years of education,

take an extensive exam, and complete continuing legal education (CLE) requirements.

5. **Nonlawyers are not regulated by the Florida Bar.**[7] There is no attorney-client relationship, and no accountability for complaints or lawsuits. Lawyers must behave in accordance with rules regulating their practice and can be disciplined for failing to do so.

6. **No Legal Malpractice Insurance.** Only a licensed attorney is entitled to have legal malpractice insurance. If the Medicaid planning fails, and there is no malpractice insurance, the applicant stands to lose his or her life savings and the facility may be stuck with a large unpaid bill.

7. The unlicensed practice of law is a **felony in the state of Florida.**

8. **Confidentiality.** Lawyers have an ethical responsibility to maintain confidentiality. Nonlawyers do not.[8]

CHAPTER 2

FLORIDA SUPREME COURT RULES THAT MEDICAID PLANNING BY NONLAWYERS IS THE UNLICENSED PRACTICE OF LAW

In January 2015, the Florida Supreme Court issued an Advisory Opinion explaining exactly what activities are considered to be the unlicensed practice of law as it pertains to Medicaid planning.

Except for licensed attorneys, anyone who advises a Florida Medicaid applicant on how to structure their income and assets in order to become eligible for Medicaid benefits is practicing law without a license.[9]

Why did the Florida Supreme Court make this ruling? To protect the public. Individuals who practice law without the proper training, licensure, insurance and accountability can bring great harm to seniors, their families and caregivers.

What is the unlicensed practice of law in Florida?

UPL mostly occurs when a person who is not a licensed attorney provides legal services to another. In the case of nursing homes and assisted living facilities, this can occur when facility employees get involved in preparing a patient's legal documents or advising them on how to transfer or structure assets to qualify for Medicaid.

Social workers and caseworkers have a good understanding of the Medicaid program. They often assist with preparing Medicaid applications for patients. <u>Helping a resident fill out State of Florida Medicaid application forms is not UPL.</u>

However, service providers who work closely with seniors and/or the disabled may find themselves assisting with the preparation of legal documents such as Durable Powers of Attorney (DPOA), Qualified Income Trusts (QITs) or other estate planning documents. These actions can actually prevent that person's chances of qualifying for Medicaid.[10]

Four things a nonlawyer Medicaid planner cannot do

The Advisory Opinion spells out what a nonlawyer may not do. **A nonlawyer individual may not:**[11]

1. **Draft personal service contracts.**
   Also known as Family Caregiver Agreements, these contracts help the senior qualify for Medicaid benefits by reducing his or her reportable assets. The contract is between the Medicaid applicant and a designated caregiver, often a family member. The senior pays the caregiver to provide personal services that are not

provided by the nursing home or assisted living facility. Services might include assistance with activities of daily living, attending doctors' appointments, meeting with attorneys, paying bills and bookkeeping.

2. **Determine the need for, prepare, fund and execute a Qualified Income Trust (QIT).**
   This includes gathering the information necessary to complete the trust. The Qualified Income Trust is an irrevocable trust created with the applicant's income in order to meet Medicaid eligibility requirements. Each month, an amount of the senior's income is placed into the account for as long as Medicaid is needed.

3. **Sell or provide forms for Personal Service Contracts or Qualified Income Trust forms or kits in the area of Medicaid planning.**
   Some nonlawyer Medicaid planners may sell or provide QIT or personal service contract forms to residents. Providing these forms is UPL.

4. **Give legal advice regarding the implementation of Florida law to obtain Medicaid benefits.**
   This includes advising an individual on the appropriate legal strategies available for spending down and restructuring assets, developing a plan to structure or spend those assets, drafting legal documents to execute the plan, and assisting the client in correctly executing the legal plan.

What can a nonlawyer legally do regarding Medicaid planning activities?

A nonlawyer may assist a Medicaid applicant with the preparation of the actual Medicaid application itself, as it is authorized by federal law.

In addition, Florida Department of Children and Families (DCF) employees who are nonlawyers may legally assist Medicaid applicants with the application process. DCF employees may also inform Medicaid applicants about Medicaid.

Who is allowed to practice law in Florida?

As a rule, in order to practice law in Florida a person must be a member of The Florida Bar.

A few exceptions, established by rule or law, may allow limited practice in Florida without being admitted:[12]

- Emeritus Attorney Pro Bono Participation Program
- Authorized Legal Aid Practitioner Rule
- Foreign Legal Consultancy Rule
- Authorized House Counsel Rule
- Military Legal Assistance Counsel Rule

These exceptions are all limited in scope of practice.

What are the civil and criminal penalties for UPL in Florida?

Civil Cases

Reports of unlicensed practice of law are investigated by UPL committees. Florida Bar prosecutions are filed with the Supreme Court of Florida and trials are held before judges, called referees, appointed by the court. The Florida Bar acts as prosecutor in unlicensed practice of law cases. The Florida Bar cases are civil in nature.[13]

Criminal Cases

Engaging in the unlicensed practice of law in Florida is also a crime. It is a **third degree felony** in Florida, punishable by up to five years in prison. For this reason, the State Attorney also has the power to bring criminal charges against an individual for practicing law without a license.[14]

Penalties and sanctions for UPL violations that are available to enforcement authorities include:[15]

- civil injunctions
- criminal fines
- prison sentence
- civil contempt
- restitution
- civil fines

Other remedies may be available, and most jurisdictions have several available remedies and all can be combined.

In addition, the effects or consequences of UPL may result in additional criminal charges depending on the type of activity and the damages to the victim.

CHAPTER 3

NURSING HOME REFERRAL LIABILITY

It is very common for seniors who need help qualifying for Medicaid to accept referrals from trusted sources—such as family, friends, social workers, nursing home administrators and hospital discharge planners. The trouble is, these referrals are frequently to nonlawyer Medicaid planners.[16]

In some cases, referrals are made without the knowledge or awareness of the nursing home resident; other times, the resident assumes they have no choice, and must use the referred planner.

Both the source (nursing facility or employee) who refers the nonlawyer for Medicaid planning purposes, and the senior resident (or their legal representative) who retains the nonlawyer, should be aware of the possible severe consequences and possible illegality of their actions—however intentional or unintentional their actions may be.

According to Florida Statute 777.011:[17]

"Whoever commits any criminal offense ... or aids, abets, counsels, hires, or otherwise procures such offense to be committed ... is a principal in the first degree and may be charged, convicted, and punished as such, whether he or she is or is not actually or constructively present at the commission of such offense."

Anyone who works closely with Florida's seniors—and especially seniors in need of Medicaid planning—must be aware of the ramifications of referring legal work to nonlawyer Medicaid planners for those in your care.

Know how to protect yourselves and your facility from the risks of exposure to liability.

What are possible legal consequences of negligent referral?

Referring Medicaid cases to a nonlawyer Medicaid planner can lead to potential liability for the nursing home and its employees.

> **Example:** Carmela holds valid durable power of attorney for her father Xavier, who is a resident of a skilled nursing facility in Santa Rosa County, Florida.
>
> Instead of hiring an attorney to help Xavier qualify for Medicaid, Carmela hires a very likable insurance salesman named Tony, who is holding himself out as a Medicaid Planning Specialist.
>
> Tony was recommended by the nursing facility to Carmela. Tony was paying the nursing home representative $200 for each client referral he received from the facility.

Tony is only somewhat familiar with Florida Medicaid rules. The legal advice he gives to Xavier and Carmella, and the legal documents he draws up, are insufficient and do not restructure Xavier's assets correctly. Tony's Medicaid planning for Xavier fails and the Medicaid program denies Xavier's application.

Carmel now must find and hire an experienced Elder Law attorney to fix the damage caused by Tony. By this time, Xavier owes the nursing home $57,600 for the cost of his care for the past 7 months.

Carmela sues Tony for the $57,600 owed to the facility, but she quickly finds out that Tony has no legal malpractice insurance. Carmela also discovers there are multiple other lawsuits pending against Tony because of failed Medicaid cases, In fact, Tony has filed bankruptcy to protect himself against the pending lawsuits. Unfortunately Carmela realizes that Tony will not be able to make Carmela or her father whole.

To add to Carmela's woes, at the time of her father's admittance to the nursing home, she had signed an admissions document that made her personally liable for any unpaid bill at the nursing home. Carmella is personally liable for the $57,600 owed to the facility.

Carmela contacts an attorney who concentrates his practice in negligent referral lawsuits. After listening to the facts, the attorney advises Carmela to sue the nursing home under a theory of negligent referral.

A lawsuit is filed against the nursing home, and the facility decides to settle the case out of court, because the corporate owners realize that the nursing home employee was clearly negligent in referring Carmela to Tony, who was not qualified to handle the Medicaid case.

The nursing home also fired the employee, because she negligently referred Carmela to Tony, and because she accepted $200 payment from Tony as a kickback.[18]

Be on the safe side! Protect your own legal rights.

- Do not refer elders who need asset restructuring or qualified income trusts to nonlawyer Medicaid planners. While you may assume a Medicaid advisor or planning company is legally qualified to advise residents of the nursing facility in these matters, this can be disastrous for the resident when you are wrong.
- Do not have a contractual relationship with nonlawyer Medicaid planners, where the facility pays the planner for legal work, or gets some form of kickback or reward for referrals.
- Make sure the nursing home resident is free to choose his or her legal advisor.
- Refer the senior and his or her family to the Florida Bar (www.floridabar.org) where the senior may seek out a qualified elder law attorney. An experienced elder law attorney will counsel the senior and family about the full range of long-term care issues, Medicaid planning legal options to protect assets, and all possible consequences and costs relevant to the senior's circumstances.
- Finally, avoid drafting or executing any legal document or contract yourself for seniors or family members; do not advise the senior or family members about what forms to get or how to fill them out.

CHAPTER 4

WHO REGULATES NONLAWYER MEDICAID PLANNING IN FLORIDA?

Nonlawyer Medicaid planning is a completely unregulated business. As the Florida Supreme Court reaffirms in the 2015 Advisory Opinion, there is no state or federal agency to license and regulate Medicaid planners. Likewise there are no educational, testing or advertising requirements.

While someone might hold a professional license to sell annuities or practice financial planning, that license and impressive title does not authorize the person to practice Medicaid planning legal activities.[19]

Insurance agents and financial planners are within the law to sell annuities and life insurance, and to serve as a designated representative for a Florida Medicaid applicants. However, the drafting of legal documents, such as personal services contracts and qualified income trusts, and giving legal advice on using Florida law to obtain Medicaid benefits, crosses the line into the unlicensed practice of law.

When a case of nonlawyer Medicaid planning becomes a matter of UPL, the Florida Bar may step in.

The Florida Bar, as an arm of the Supreme Court, is the state authority charged with investigating matters pertaining to the unlicensed practice of law and prosecuting offenders. All complaints alleging unlicensed practice of law must be signed, in writing, and under oath.

In order for UPL to be managed, somebody must report it.[20]

To compound the problem, the Florida Bar will not open a UPL case without someone filing a UPL complaint with the Bar.

The public is rarely reporting cases of UPL. Nobody wants to be a whistleblower. The stigma of snitching creates a sort of "code of silence" from the shame of being labeled an informant. In addition, long term care residents and their families may fear retaliation by a facility who makes a referral.

The justification for filing an official UPL complaint – *snitching* if you will – lies in the intent. Informing on the unlicensed practice of law is not a self-serving endeavor, but is in the public interest.

The "Catch-22" of UPL

In effect, the Florida Bar is relying on its citizens to be the watchdogs and whistleblowers, with respect to investigating the unlicensed practice of law in Florida.

Yet few people are willing to file UPL complaints. The absence of reporting UPL in turn encourages its continuance.

We have a responsibility to one another – and it seems especially to our unsuspecting seniors and their families. Reluctance to take a legitimate case of UPL to the Florida Bar leaves these individuals in a tragically vulnerable situation.

What is our duty?

In the Florida Supreme Court Advisory Opinion, the absence of regulations imposed on nonlawyer Medicaid planners falls under the heading of HARM AND THE POTENTIAL FOR HARM.

It is our view that by reporting UPL, the higher virtue is served by respecting the well-being of others. It is acting responsibly on behalf of society to report bad behavior.

Contrary to arguments of many nonlawyer Medicaid planners, this is not a turf war between lawyers and nonlawyers. There is no effort to protect some sort of attorney monopoly on legal services, taking away "cheaper" alternatives for people who desire to go that route. Neither is this an attempt to take away conveniences for consumers. Indeed, Medicaid planning by nonlawyers may not be cheaper. Also nonlawyers do not offer alternatives as lawyers do.

The purpose of this discussion is to protect the public. It is a wakeup call to all of us. It is up to our own citizens to open up communication between the community and the Florida Bar.

It is also a matter of education. Many UPL victims are unaware they have been victimized until it is too late. They may be ashamed or embarrassed about putting their trust in the wrong hands. On the flip side, many offenders and those who unwittingly assist them are ignorant about the severity of their own actions.

As stated by the Florida Bar, "The Florida Bar unlicensed practice of law (UPL) system [is] established by the Supreme Court of Florida to protect the public against harm caused by unlicensed individuals practicing law."[21]

File a UPL complaint

How to File a UPL Complaint with the Florida Bar:

The Florida Bar provides a short form that can be completed in order to report alleged instances of UPL. The form is available for the public to download at www.floridabar.org, along with helpful information about how the process works, and what to expect.

Learn all about it here:

Florida Bar, Online Resource for the Public:

Consumer Pamphlet: Filing an Unlicensed Practice of Law Complaint

at: https://www.floridabar.org/public/consumer/pamphlet012/

Florida Bar UPL Branch Offices

The UPL department has offices in Tallahassee, Ft. Lauderdale, Miami, Orlando and Tampa. The addresses are:[22]

Tallahassee
The Florida Bar
UPL Department
651 E. Jefferson Street

Tallahassee, FL 32399-2300
(850) 561-5840

Ft. Lauderdale
The Florida Bar
UPL Department
Lake Shore Plaza II
1300 Concord Terrace, Ste. 130
Sunrise, FL 33323-2899
(954) 835-0233, ext. 4148

Miami
The Florida Bar
UPL Department
Rivergate Plaza, Ste. M100
444 Brickell Ave.
Miami, FL 33131-2404
(305) 377-4445, ext. 4218

Orlando
The Florida Bar
UPL Department
The Gateway Center
1000 Legion Place, Ste. 1625
Orlando, FL 32801
(407) 425-0473

Tampa
The Florida Bar
UPL Department
4200 George J. Bean Pkwy., Ste. 2580
Tampa, FL 33607-1496
(813) 875-9821, ext. 4323

CHAPTER 5

WHAT SORT OF TRAINING, EDUCATION AND LICENSING DO NONLAWYER MEDICAID PLANNERS HAVE?

What is the background, education and knowledge base of nonlawyer Medicaid planners?

Annuity and insurance sales agents

Annuity and insurance sales agents sell annuities, life insurance and related financial products and earn commission from the sale. There is no requirement for a college degree, but a sales agent must pass a state insurance commission exam to obtain a license to sell insurance and certain annuities.

Agents who sell securities (and variable annuities) must also be licensed as a registered representative and comply with Financial Industry Regulating Authority (FINRA) regulations.[23]

They are by definition salespersons. Their knowledge is of their financial products, and their training is how to promote and sell them.

Although insurance is a highly regulated profession, insurance agents *without a law license* have no formal training, education or licensing associated with Florida Medicaid planning law and the complex planning strategies accepted by Medicaid. For many, their only familiarity with Medicaid may be what they receive in sales brochures.

Financial planners[24, 25]

Financial planners come from many different educational and professional backgrounds.

According to the U.S. Securities and Exchange Commission:

- some financial planners charge either a fixed fee or an hourly fee for the time it takes to develop a financial plan, but don't sell investment products;
- some are paid by commissions on the products they sell;
- and others use a combination of fees and commissions.

Some financial planners have credentials like CFP (Certified Financial Planner) certification or CFA (Chartered Financial Analyst). The criteria for these are determined by the private organization that issues the credential.

FINRA does NOT approve or endorse any professional credential or designation.

As with insurance agents, a financial planner *without a law license* has no training, education or licensing associated with Florida Medicaid planning and the complex planning strategies accepted by Medicaid.

Former healthcare employees

Other nonlawyer Medicaid planners emerge from the health care industry, such as geriatric care managers, former nurses, prior DCF employees, and former nursing home employees. All have their own learned aspects of elder care, but no legal knowledge or training of the complex Medicaid planning strategies, or the preservation of assets, or the estate and income tax consequences caused by a restructuring of assets.

Planners with a public record

Nonlawyer Medicaid planners may also be **felons, disbarred attorneys, sanctioned insurance sales people or other bad actors** (as described in Chapter 6.)

CHAPTER 6

WHO ARE NONLAWYER MEDICAID PLANNERS?

Individuals and companies with no license to practice law, yet stake their claim as Florida "Medicaid planners" run the gamut.

Individuals as Medicaid planners

Public record shows that the following types of individuals have been Medicaid planners in Florida:

- annuity salesmen
- insurance salesmen
- geriatric care managers
- Florida licensed nurses
- former nursing home employees
- former DCF employees
- a disbarred attorney
- a convicted felon
- individuals with revoked insurance licenses

- an individual permanently barred from the securities industry by Financial Industry Regulatory Authority (FINRA)
- individuals permanently barred from the securities industry by the Florida Office of Financial Regulation
- a variety of other untrained and unlicensed individuals.

Medicaid planning companies

"But we work with lawyers!"

When lawyers themselves collaborate with nonlawyer Medicaid planners, more ethical and legal issues can arise. Attorneys not only run the risk of engaging in felonious activities, they risk crossing the line of the rules of professional ethics, bypassing the "duty of loyalty only to their client."

- An attorney who works with a nonlawyer Medicaid planner needs to be careful not to violate **"Confidentiality of Information"** when interacting with the nonlawyer. *See* The Florida Bar, Rules of Professional Conduct (RPC) 4-1.6. Since the nonlawyer Medicaid planner may only collect information for the purpose of filling out a Medicaid application and not to develop a Medicaid strategy or to prepare legal documents, the attorney needs to be mindful of breach of confidentiality by disclosing private and potentially sensitive information to the nonlawyer.[26]
- When the Medicaid planning company refers all or most of its Medicaid application clients to the same attorney for Medicaid planning services, the potential for a **"Conflict of Interest"** under RPC 4-1.7 exists. When the attorney is receiving substantial income from a nonlawyer Medicaid planner, it is arguable that the attorney's loyalty is to the nonlawyer and not to the client who has been referred.[27]

For these and other reasons, the Florida Supreme Court Advisory Opinion also targets Medicaid planning companies that profess to work with lawyers, where those lawyers prepare Medicaid planning documents for the company's clients.

The Florida Supreme Court determined this practice between such companies and attorneys also constitutes the unlicensed practice of law *unless:*

- the client establishes an independent attorney-client relationship with the attorney;
- payment from the client is made directly to the attorney, and
- the attorney specifically determines the legal Medicaid planning strategy and legal documents as appropriate for the client, given the client's particular factual circumstances.

In response to the Florida Supreme Court UPL advisory opinion, some non-attorney Medicaid Planners merged their entire Medicaid planning company - including all employees - with Florida law firms.

What if a non-attorney Medicaid Planner becomes an employee (paralegal) for a licensed attorney? This may still constitute UPL by the non-attorney, as well as aiding and abetting UPL by the attorney. Does this new arrangement eliminate the UPL problem for the non-attorney?

What facts should the nursing home look for?

1. Did the attorney communicate with the client?
2. Did the attorney supervise the employee's activities?
3. Did the client hire the attorney before they met the employee?
4. Did the attorney receive the larger part of the fee?

5. Did the attorney discuss Medicaid strategies with the client or split the fee with the non-attorney?

These are some of the factors to be evaluated in determining whether or not UPL and/or ethical violations may have been committed.

CHAPTER 7

EXAMPLES OF PROBLEMS CAUSED BY NONLAWYER MEDICAID PLANNERS

What is the potential for harm to the public? Nonlawyer Medicaid planners expose Florida nursing home residents to various dangers, including[28]

- the denial of Medicaid eligibility
- ineligibility penalties, costing tens or hundreds of thousands of dollars, because of wrongful transfers or purchasing unfit financial products
- exploitation of vulnerable, unsuspecting Florida citizens
- leaving seniors and their families or caregivers open to charges of Medicaid fraud
- severe or ruinous tax debts and obligations
- purchasing the wrong or erroneous financial products, or having an insufficient power of attorney — threatening or destroying a person's life savings

An example to highlight the hidden dangers: a life's savings, wiped out in months

Consider this scenario:

Alejandra contacted a nonlawyer Medicaid planner, Steve, who is a Florida licensed insurance agent who holds himself out as a "Medicaid Planning Specialist."

Alejandra's father, Armando has been a resident at an assisted living facility in Escambia County, Florida. The owner of the assisted living facility referred Alejandra to Steve. The assisted living facility can no longer meet Armando's medical needs, and Armando must now move to a skilled nursing facility.

Armando's gross monthly income is $4,000.00 per month, which includes his Social Security and a DFAS pension, from Armando's prior military service in the United States Air Force. The $4,000.00 per month in income had been just enough to pay the $3,800.00 per month bill at the assisted living facility.

However, the private pay bill at the new nursing home is going to be $9,100.00 per month, and Armando has no money saved up, and he generally only has about $1,500.00 left over in his checking account each month after paying the assisted living bill.

The insurance agent Steve tells Alejandra that he has drafted durable powers of attorney and qualified income trusts for his clients in the past, and that he has successfully obtained Medicaid benefits for nursing home residents in the past. Steve advised Alejandra that Armando will need a qualified income trust to obtain Medicaid benefits, because Armando's monthly income exceeds the $2,250 income cap.

Steve quotes a fee of $3,800.00 to draft a durable power of attorney, a qualified income trust, and submit the Medicaid application for Armando.

Steve is also a Notary Public. Steve prepares the durable power of attorney for Armando, and goes to the nursing home to visit with Armando and execute the durable power of attorney. Steve properly executes the power of attorney with two witnesses, and then sets up an appointment with Alejandra, who Armando has named as his attorney-in-fact in his newly signed durable power of attorney.

Steve then prepares a qualified income trust, and has Alejandra sign the income trust in the presence of two witnesses. Steve tells Alejandra that he has provided these exact same services for many Medicaid applicants in the past, and all of his cases have been approved.

After Armando's Medicaid is submitted to DCF, the Medicaid application is denied. Unfortunately, Steve was not aware that Florida adopted a new power of attorney statute on October 1, 2011. Steve continued to use the same power of attorney document after October 1, 2011 that he had been providing to clients for the past few years. Under the new power of attorney statute, a "general grant of authority" is no longer effective, and in order to establish an irrevocable trust, a separate provision in the durable power document authorizing the establishment of the trust needed to be initialed or signed by Armando.

Because Steve was not aware of the new power of attorney statute and his power of attorney form was insufficient to establish the qualified income trust, DCF denied the Medicaid application. By the time the decision was issued by the DCF caseworker in Armando's Medicaid case, three months had passed, and the unpaid bill in the nursing home exceeded $27,000.00.

Neither Armando nor Alejandra had sufficient funds available to pay for the unpaid private pay bill in the nursing home, and when the Medicaid case was denied, the nursing facility issued a discharge notice to Armando, due to his failure to pay the bill.[29]

CHAPTER 8

DOES A NONLAWYER MEDICAID PLANNER HAVE LEGAL MALPRACTICE INSURANCE?

No. By definition, only an attorney licensed to practice law would be entitled to have legal malpractice insurance.

If an annuity sales person only holds a license with the Florida Department of Insurance (or no license at all), that person would not be able to purchase legal malpractice insurance.

The financial stakes are very high in Medicaid cases. The private pay rate, including incidentals, often exceeds $8,000.00 per month. Over the course of one year, that adds up to $96,000.

Who will make the client or nursing home facility whole, if the nonlawyer Medicaid planning fails?

If the Medicaid planning fails, and there is no malpractice insurance, who is able to compensate the exploited Medicaid applicant, or the nursing home or assisted living facility? Not the insurance agent or an unlicensed financial planner.[30]

Victims who have been financially damaged by a nonlawyer improperly engaging in UPL in Florida have a right to be compensated, and may take legal action to recover damages. But from whom?

The Florida Bar is responsible for investigating and prosecuting the unlicensed practice of law in Florida. See **Chapter 4** for information about filing a UPL complaint.

CHAPTER 9

WHAT WILL HAPPEN IF A NONLAWYER MEDICAID PLANNER TAKES MONEY FROM THE NURSING HOME RESIDENT?

Serious liabilities may lurk for long term care facilities and employees affiliated with nonlawyer Medicaid planners.

When a non-lawyer Medicaid planner's actions result in the nursing home resident's personal financial harm and/or denial of Medicaid eligibility, this can become a matter of **financial exploitation** of the resident.

Depending on the case, the facility in which the resident is staying and/ or employee who referred the nonlawyer Medicaid planner may be held accountable. There may be a case for negligence under the doctrine of negligent referral, a breach in duty of reasonable care or causation of financial exploitation.

Don't let this happen! Here are common scenarios:

1.) If the nursing home or employee refers a resident to a nonlawyer Medicaid planner, that nonlawyer has "loyalties" to the nursing home as well as to the nursing home resident. That is a conflict of interest: who will the nonlawyer Medicaid planner take care of?

2.) If the nursing home resident pays money to the nonlawyer in exchange for Medicaid planning services, the nonlawyer Medicaid planner has a business relationship with the resident. If the nursing home or employee that refers the nonlawyer Medicaid planner to the nursing home resident gets a *referral fee* or *kickback*, there could be civil or criminal liability. **See Chapters 12 and 13 for more about kickbacks, fees and solicitations.**

3.) Suppose no one gets caught? A nonlawyer Medicaid planner may get huge commissions or payouts while causing expensive problems for the senior resident and the nursing home, not to mention the compromised families and community.

- Has the nonlawyer Medicaid "advisor" charged the senior resident a large sum of money for wrong legal advice, invalid trusts or other flawed transfer or spend down of assets?
- Has the nonlawyer made a small fortune by selling the senior resident an annuity he or she does not even need? The senior has no guarantee that the financial product he or she purchased with personal savings was even necessary or appropriate for Medicaid planning.
- Did the nonlawyer's incorrect legal advice result in disastrous and unexpected tax consequences for the senior?

CHAPTER 10

AHCA, ELDER ABUSE, ELDER EXPLOITATION, AS IT RELATES TO UPL

The **Florida Agency for Health Care Administration (AHCA)** is very involved with Florida nursing home and long term care facilities, and Florida Medicaid proceedings and administration. This includes all Medicaid planning activities.

Florida AHCA is responsible for:

- administrating the Florida Medicaid program,
- licensure and regulation of Florida's health facilities and
- providing information to Floridians about the quality of care they receive.

What is elder abuse and exploitation with regards to Medicaid planning by nonlawyers?

Exploitation generally refers to the loss of a person's assets and property, money or income. In the case of UPL, this refers to types of harm caused by nonlawyer Medicaid planners which includes denial of Medicaid eligibility, exploitation, catastrophic or severe tax liability, and the purchase of inappropriate financial products threatening or destroying client's life savings.[31]

The **Florida Department of Children and Families (DCF)** further explains Elder Exploitation as follows: [32]

> Adult exploitation means a person who stands in a position of trust and confidence with a vulnerable adult knowingly, by deception or intimidation, obtains or uses, or endeavors to obtain or use, a vulnerable adult's funds, assets, or property with the intent to temporarily or permanently deprive a vulnerable adult of the use, benefit, or possession of the funds, assets, or property for the benefit of someone other than the vulnerable adult.

> *OR*

> That a person who knows or should know that the vulnerable adult lacks the capacity to consent, obtains or uses, or endeavors to obtain or use, the vulnerable adult's funds, assets, or property with the intent to temporarily or permanently deprive the vulnerable adult of the use, benefit, or possession of the funds, assets, or property for the benefit of someone other than the vulnerable adult.

Florida Statute 825.103—*Exploitation of an elderly person or disabled adult; penalties*—states the following people can be held liable for elder exploitation[33]

- Someone in a position of trust with the elderly person or disabled adult
- A person who has a business relationship with the elderly person or disabled adult
- Guardians
- Trustees
- Agents under a power of attorney
- Caregivers

Financial exploitation is a form of elder abuse.

Elder abuse in Florida is a felony. The failure to report abuse that has occurred also may be a crime.

Florida statute 825.103 breaks down the financial exploitation felony and penalty potential:

825.103 (3)(a) If the funds, assets, or property involved in the exploitation of the elderly person or disabled adult is valued at **$50,000 or more**, the offender commits a **felony of the first degree**, punishable as provided in s. 775.082, s. 775.083, or s. 775.084.

(b) If the funds, assets, or property involved in the exploitation of the elderly person or disabled adult is valued at $10,000 or more, but less than $50,000, the offender commits a **felony of the second degree**, punishable as provided in s. 775.082, s. 775.083, or s. 775.084.

> (c) If the funds, assets, or property involved in the exploitation of an elderly person or disabled adult is valued at **less than $10,000**, the offender commits a **felony of the third degree**, punishable as provided in s. 775.082, s. 775.083, or s. 775.084.

I have an elder abuse concern or complaint. Who can I call?

The following contact information is provided by the Florida Agency for Health Care Administration (AHCA)[34]

Bureau of Medicaid Program Integrity
1-888-419-3456
Medicaid Program Integrity audits and investigates providers suspected of overbilling or defrauding Florida's Medicaid program. If you feel that you have been charged for services that should be paid for by Medicaid, or if someone billed Medicaid for services that were not provided, this unit will investigate Medicaid billing practices to determine if they were appropriate. To report a complaint, please call toll-free 1-888-419-3456, or go to the Agency web site at http://ahca.myflorida.com/Executive/Inspector_General/medicaid.shtml.

Medicaid Fraud Control Unit
1-866-966-7226
Medicaid fraud means an intentional deception or misrepresentation made by a health care provider with the knowledge that the deception could result in some unauthorized benefit to him or herself or some other person. It includes any act that constitutes fraud under applicable federal or state law as it relates to Medicaid. To report suspected Medicaid fraud, please call the Attorney General toll-free 1-866-966-7226.

Under Florida law, you may be entitled to a reward for providing information after a criminal case has resulted in a fine, penalty, or forfeiture of property. The amount of the reward may be up to 25 percent of the amount recovered, or a maximum of $500,000 per case.

The Florida Department of Children and Families Abuse Hotline #1-800-96-ABUSE
The Florida Department of Children and Families accepts reports 24 hours a day, 7 days a week.

CHAPTER 11

DOES A NURSING HOME HAVE A FIDUCIARY RESPONSIBILITY TO ITS RESIDENTS?

One might think at least in principle that fiduciary responsibilities exist for the nursing home. But under Florida law that is not the case.

The answer is based on case law - and **Florida has not recognized a fiduciary relationship between a nursing home and its residents.** There are no opinions in the jurisprudence of the State of Florida recognizing such a fiduciary relationship.[35, 36]

To recover damages from the alleged Breach of Fiduciary Duty, the plaintiff must prove (1) the existence of a fiduciary duty; (2) breach of the fiduciary duty; and (3) damages caused by the breach.[37]

While Florida has recognized that fiduciary relationships exist in the context of the physician-patient relationship, therapist-patient relationship and counselor-patient relationships, no such fiduciary relationship has been extended to the nursing home-resident relationship. [38]

And while the nursing home is undoubtedly under a duty to provide care and treatment to its residents, the relationships between the nursing staff and the residents is not such that they are required to give advice to the residents. It is undisputed that such advice is limited to the relationship between the residents and their physicians. To hold otherwise would expand the confines of the traditional fiduciary relationship well beyond that envisioned by the Supreme Court of Florida.[39]

What is a fiduciary responsibility, or duty?

Under Florida law, a fiduciary duty is a legal and ethical relationship created when a person places special trust and confidence in another person to take care of his or her money, assets and financial affairs and transactions.

The fiduciary is obliged to act in the other party's best interest. The fiduciary's actions must be free of conflicts of interest and self-dealing.

A breach of fiduciary duties happens when the fiduciary acts in their own interest and not in the interest of the client. They act to gain or obtain some benefit at the expense of the client.

So who are considered "fiduciaries" with regards to nursing home residents?

Generally the following individuals or entities may have legal duty to act as fiduciary:

- agents under a power of attorney
- court-appointed guardians
- trustees of a trust
- executors of a will
- VA fiduciaries

- Social Security representative payees
- professionals with the obligation to act in their clients best interests (e.g., attorneys, financial advisors, CPAs, banks, family members)

Protecting the residents in your care

In the relationship between a nursing home and an elderly resident, the resident is dependent upon the services provided by the nursing home. The resident is also dependent upon the staff's knowledge of the healthcare system, the staff's access to their privileged information, and the staff's ability to influence decisions that affect the patient.

If the resident has a fiduciary, the facility should obtain and keep on file documentation of the fiduciary's authority. Examples of documentation involving a fiduciary's authority include:[40]

- trust documents
- power of attorney
- court designations naming a guardian
- payee authorization for a Social Security representative
- VA fiduciary appointments
- Letters of Guardianship

A final point to consider:

Although no legal opinions exist that identify a fiduciary relationship between a nursing home and its residents, it is in everyone's best interest to avoid actions that could be so interpreted. A prominent example is a nursing home that refers Medicaid applicants to a nonlawyer Medicaid planner, especially for kickbacks or rewards. In certain cases this could place the nursing home in a situation of abusing its "position of trust and confidence" as described in Chapter 10.

CHAPTER 12

CAN THE NURSING HOME GET IN TROUBLE IF THE NURSING HOME EMPLOYEES KNOW THAT THE NONLAWYER MEDICAID PLANNER IS ENGAGING IN UPL?

Yes, it is possible. According to Florida Statute 777.011, (and as stated in Chapter 3):[41]

Both referral sources and seniors who retain a nonlawyer for Medicaid planning purposes should be aware of the possible illegality of their actions, however unwitting or intentional their actions may be.

> "Whoever commits any criminal offense ... or aids, abets, counsels, hires, or otherwise procures such offense to be committed ... is a principal in the first degree and may be charged, convicted, and punished as such, whether he or she is or is not actually or constructively present at the commission of such offense."

In addition to state mandatory reporting laws, federal law requires long-term care facilities that receive at least $10,000 in federal funds during the preceding year to report suspected crimes against a resident to state survey agencies and to local law enforcement.

Specifically, the law requires that the owner, operator, employee, manager, agent, or contractor of a covered facility report "any reasonable suspicion of a crime," as defined by local law, committed against a resident of, or someone receiving care from, the facility.[42] [43]

Could a nursing home employee referring to a nonlawyer who engages in UPL result in fines?

Yes. In cases in which the employee or nursing home has a business interest (i.e. receives a kick-back or financial reward) with the nonlawyer to which he or she makes referrals, certain Florida anti-kickback statutes may be imposed.

It is a good idea for nursing home staff and operators to have an understanding of the following Florida statutes regulating bribes, kickbacks, solicitations and rebates as it pertains to Medicaid planning activities and referring residents to nonlawyer Medicaid planners.

Chapter 400 - NURSING HOMES AND RELATED HEALTH CARE FACILITIES

Fla. Stat. 400.17 Bribes, kickbacks, certain solicitations prohibited.—

(1) As used in this section, the term:

    (a) "Bribe" means any consideration corruptly given, received, promised, solicited, or offered to any individual with intent or purpose to influence the performance of any act or omission.

    (b) "Kickback" means that part of the payment for items or services which is returned to the payor by the provider of such items or services with the intent or purpose to induce the payor to purchase the items or services from the provider.

(2) Whoever furnishes items or services directly or indirectly to a nursing home resident and solicits, offers, or receives any:

    (a) Kickback or bribe in connection with the furnishing of such items or services or the making or receipt of such payment; or

    (b) Return of part of an amount given in payment for referring any such individual to another person for the furnishing of such items or services; is guilty of a misdemeanor of the first degree, punishable as provided in s. 775.082 or by fine not exceeding $5,000, or both.

(3) No person shall, in connection with the solicitation of contributions to nursing homes, willfully misrepresent or mislead anyone, by any manner, means, practice, or device whatsoever, to believe that the receipts of such solicitation will be used for charitable purposes, if such is not the fact.

(4) Solicitation of contributions of any kind in a threatening, coercive, or unduly forceful manner by or on behalf of a nursing home by any agent, employee, owner, or representative of a nursing home shall be grounds for denial, suspension, or revocation of the license for any nursing home on behalf of which such contributions were solicited.

(5) The admission, maintenance, or treatment of a nursing home resident whose care is supported in whole or in part by state funds may not be made conditional upon the receipt of any manner of contribution or donation from any person. However, this may not be construed to prohibit the offer or receipt of contributions or donations to a nursing home which are not related to the care of a specific resident. Contributions solicited or received in violation of this subsection shall be grounds for denial, suspension, or revocation of a license for any nursing home on behalf of which such contributions were solicited.

Fla. Stat. 400.176   Rebates prohibited; penalties.—

(1) It is unlawful for any person to pay or receive any commission, bonus, kickback or rebate or engage in any split-fee arrangement in any form whatsoever with any physician, surgeon, organization, agency or person either directly indirectly, for residents referred to a nursing home licensed under this part.

(2) The agency shall enforce subsection (1). In the case of an entity not licensed by the agency, administrative penalties may include:

(a) A fine not to exceed $5,000; and
(b) If applicable, a recommendation by the agency to the appropriate licensing board that disciplinary action be taken.

CHAPTER 13

Is it against the Law for a Nursing Home Employee to be Paid a Fee to Refer Medicaid Cases to a Nonlawyer Medicaid Planner?

When facilities or employees receive rewards for referring to nonlawyers, things take a turn for the worse. Under Florida law, "bribes, kickbacks, and certain solicitations are prohibited." The nursing home that engages in such activity may be subject to civil liability or even criminal penalties.

But imagine how easy it is for an overwhelmed family, who is not sure where to turn for advice, to take the guidance of someone they trust, such as a spokesperson for the nursing home where a senior family member now resides.

> **Nursing home:** *"Go see this Medicaid planning advisor, they're the best! They'll take good care of your Dad and help him get benefits."*

> **Family:** *"Thanks, we weren't sure who to call. We'll go see them today!"*

It is reckless and ill-considered for employees of nursing homes or other senior care facilities to refer legal work to nonlawyer Medicaid planners. Who will be found liable when something goes wrong?

Much blame will be cast on the nursing home or facility for giving improper guidance to the patient. At the very least, such exposure leads to disrepute and bad public relations.

Florida Statute 400.17—Nursing Homes and Related Health Care Facilities; Bribes, kickbacks, certain solicitations prohibited:[44]

(1) As used in this section, the term:

  (a) "Bribe" means any consideration corruptly given, received, promised, solicited, or offered to any individual with intent or purpose to influence the performance of any act or omission.
  (b) "Kickback" means that part of the payment for items or services which is returned to the payor by the provider of such items or services with the intent or purpose to induce the payor to purchase the items or services from the provider.

(2) Whoever furnishes items or services directly or indirectly to a nursing home resident and solicits, offers, or receives any:

  (a) Kickback or bribe in connection with the furnishing of such items or services or the making or receipt of such payment; or
  (b) Return of part of an amount given in payment for referring any such individual to another person for the furnishing of such items or services; is guilty of a misdemeanor of the first degree, punishable as provided in s. 775.082 or by fine not exceeding $5,000, or both.

(3) No person shall, in connection with the solicitation of contributions to nursing homes, willfully misrepresent or mislead anyone, by any manner, means, practice, or device whatsoever, to believe that the receipts of such solicitation will be used for charitable purposes, if such is not the fact.

(4) Solicitation of contributions of any kind in a threatening, coercive, or unduly forceful manner by or on behalf of a nursing home by any agent, employee, owner, or representative of a nursing home shall be grounds for denial, suspension, or revocation of the license for any nursing home on behalf of which such contributions were solicited.

(5) The admission, maintenance, or treatment of a nursing home resident whose care is supported in whole or in part by state funds may not be made conditional upon the receipt of any manner of contribution or donation from any person. ... Contributions solicited or received in violation of this subsection shall be grounds for denial, suspension, or revocation of a license for any nursing home on behalf of which such contributions were solicited.

CHAPTER 14

WHAT TYPE OF FEES DO NONLAWYER MEDICAID PLANNERS CHARGE FOR THEIR SERVICES?

Commissioned-Based Medicaid Planning Fees

Some nonlawyer Medicaid planners are compensated when they sell annuities. These individuals target seniors who exceed Medicaid eligibility limits. A senior purchases an annuity from the planner in order to fall within Medicaid asset limits, and the Medicaid planner takes a commission.

The commissions associated with a Medicaid-qualifying annuity can be substantial. An annuity sales person has a strong financial incentive to try to induce a Medicaid applicant to put as much money as possible into the annuity, because the size of the commission is related to the size of the annuity.[45]

Nonlawyers are not required to disclose the commissions they receive. Therefore, rarely will nonlawyer Medicaid planners disclose the commissions they receive for the financial products they sell.

Commission plus Fees

Some nonlawyer Medicaid planners advise consumers on Medicaid laws and services for a fee, and then *also* recommend a "Medicaid friendly" annuity to the same client and earn a commission (possibly an undisclosed commission) on the sale of the annuity.[46] Often because of this, the goal of the Medicaid planning services is to get the resident to buy commission-generating financial products, not improve the resident's quality of life.

Medicaid Application Fees

In addition to earning commissions on financial products sold to Medicaid applicants, nonlawyer Medicaid planners typically charge a fee to prepare and make the application to the Florida Department of Children and Families for the Medicaid applicant. Fees quoted by these types of planners are often *equal to or higher than* fees charged by attorneys who practice in Medicaid planning.[47] When combined with undisclosed commissions, the amount ultimately received by nonlawyers can be significantly more than the fees of an attorney.

CHAPTER 15

DOES WORKING WITH A NONLAWYER MEDICAID PLANNER INCREASE THE NURSING HOME'S UNCOLLECTIBLE ACCOUNTS RECEIVABLE?

Uncollectable accounts receivable are debts that have no chance of being paid. When Medicaid planning by a nonlawyer fails for an elder resident, how will the nursing home be paid for services rendered?

Questions that need to be asked when nonlawyer Medicaid planning fails:

- Are unpaid nursing home bills the result of financial exploitation of the resident by a nonlawyer Medicaid planner?
- Did the actions of the nonlawyer lead to Medicaid ineligibility?

If the answer to these questions is *Yes*, then the nursing home's uncollectable accounts receivable is greatly affected as a result of working with a Medicaid advisor who is not an attorney. The next question is: Who will pay the bill?

- Unpaid care can be tens to hundreds of thousands of dollars;
- The family cannot possibly pay these exorbitant costs to the nursing home;
- With no malpractice insurance, and if no available assets, the nonlawyer cannot compensate the nursing home;
- The Medicaid program is not paying because of ineligibility.

When a nursing home works with or strongly encourages residents to use a nonlawyer Medicaid planner, a nursing home can be stuck with huge uncollectable accounts receivable.

So, how would you collect a judgment from a nonlawyer with no insurance or assets? The following chapter explains.

CHAPTER 16

HOW WOULD YOU COLLECT A JUDGMENT FROM A NONLAWYER WITH NO INSURANCE OR ASSETS?

What are the realities when nursing homes engage in relationships with nonlawyer Medicaid planners and things go wrong?

The following is a simplified example:

A nonlawyer's Medicaid planning strategies have failed for a resident of the facility. Because of incompetent Medicaid planning efforts, the elderly resident is now ineligible for Medicaid benefits and is facing discharge because she cannot pay the bill. By now the nursing home is in arrears for $60,000 in Medicaid payments.

A UPL complaint is filed by the nursing home, and the nonlawyer Medicaid planner is found to have engaged in the unlicensed practice of law.

The court finds that the planner is responsible for reimbursing the nursing home this money. The court enters a money judgment against the planner.

A Final Judgement is signed by the judge, and the next step is judgement collection.

There are three basic scenarios that may happen:

1. If the nonlawyer Medicaid planner is a solvent business, the Medicaid planner may actually pay voluntarily.

2. If the nonlawyer Medicaid planner is a solvent business that **refuses to pay** the judgment, the nursing facility turns to law enforcement to step in. There are different methods that could be used to collect on a money judgment. The most basic ways include

   • Garnishment
   • Execution and levy

3. But, as it so often happens, the nonlawyer Medicaid planner has no resources the nursing home can go after. The planner has no malpractice insurance, no available income, no assets or real estate to levy. How will the nursing home get the money it is due? The facility is going to have a very tough, if not impossible, time collecting on the judgement.

And if the planner is a fly-by-night operation with no central office or locatable base, executing the judgment becomes highly unlikely.

To make matters even worse, a nonlawyer Medicaid planner may be able to file bankruptcy and discharge the liability protecting any future assets or incomes from collections.

Everybody loses: The nursing home, the elder resident and family, the Medicaid program and by extension, the taxpayers all lose. Everyone except possibly the nonlawyer Medicaid planner who gets away with it.

SUMMARY

RESPONDING AS A COMMUNITY

This book is part of an extensive effort to protect Florida seniors from financial exploitation through prevention and awareness. As a community of concerned professionals, we must all work to increase public awareness about unlicensed individuals who engage in Medicaid planning, but shouldn't.

Thankfully, with the Florida Supreme Court 2015 advisory opinion, several Medicaid planning acts by nonlawyers are now determined to be the unlicensed practice of law. This brings much protection for our elders and other vulnerable Medicaid applicants.

But as some nonlawyer Medicaid planning "experts" and companies cease their wrongful activities, others snub the law and continue to flim flam those who are vulnerable. This is happening now, whether in secret or openly.

Nursing homes and assisted living facilities must stand at the front line, and stay vigilant to the dangers of Medicaid planners who are not attorneys.

With your help and understanding, we can build a culture of awareness and cooperation where it is safe and expected to protect our seniors and prevent them from financial exploitation and abuse.

Remember:

Go To: **Florida Bar, Online Resource For the Public:**

Consumer Pamphlet: Filing An Unlicensed Practice Of Law Complaint

at: https://www.floridabar.org/public/consumer/pamphlet012/

ABOUT THE AUTHORS

John R. Frazier, J.D., LL.M.

John R. Frazier graduated Cum Laude from Hampden-Sydney College in Virginia with a B.A. in Economics in 1986. He received his Master's Degree in Business Administration from Virginia Tech in 1994; graduated Cum Laude from the University of Toledo, College of Law in 1997; and received his LL.M. in Taxation from the University of Florida, College of Law in 1998.

John is licensed to practice Law in both Florida and Georgia, and he practices primarily in the fields of Elder Law, Medicaid Planning, Veterans Benefits Law, Estate Planning, Asset Protection, Taxation, and Business Organizations.

John is a member of the National Academy of Elder Law Attorneys, the Academy of Florida Elder Law Attorneys and the Florida Bar Elder Law Section. John is admitted to practice before the United States Court of Appeals for Veterans Claims, and he is accredited by the Veterans Administration to assist VA claimants present, prepare and prosecute claims with the VA.

As the son of a physician and military officer, and with four brothers, John traveled widely in the U.S.A. and abroad while growing up. John's exposure to different cultures has created a lifelong interest in learning about other regions of the world. His current interests include the study of Latin America, Spanish music, Italian music and reading.

John R. Frazier can be reached through his website:

www.EstateLegalPlanning.com

Leonard E. Mondschein, J.D., LL.M., CELA, CAP

Leonard E. Mondschein, J.D., LL.M., CELA, CAP, is a shareholder in The Elder Law Center of Mondschein and Mondschein, P.A. with offices in Miami and Aventura, Florida. He is Board Certified by the Florida Bar in Elder Law and Wills, Trusts and Estates and is a former adjunct professor of law at the University of Miami School of Law for the LL.M. program in Estate Planning. He is a Certified Elder Law Attorney by The National Elder Law Foundation, the only national Elder Law certification recognized by the ABA, and is a member of The Council of Advanced Practitioners (CAP).

Mr. Mondschein serves on the Board of Directors of The National Academy of Elder Law Attorneys. He received his Juris Doctor degree from the New England Law and his Masters of Law degree from New York University. He is Past Chair of the Elder Law Section of the Florida Bar, and is Past President of the Estate Planning Council of Greater Miami and is Past President of the South Dade Estate Planning Council, as well as Past President of the Academy of Florida Elder Law Attorneys.

Mr. Mondschein also served on the Board of Directors for the Alliance for Aging in Miami-Dade County, served as Chairman of the Special Needs Trust Committee of the Elder Law Section of the Florida Bar and is a Member Emeritus of the Pubic Policy Task Force. He has served on several steering committees for the National Academy of Elder Law Attorney's Institutes and Symposiums as well as served on their Medicaid Task force. He presently serves as Chair of the National Academy of Elder

Law Attorney's Practice Development/Practice Management Section and serves as an Editor of The NAELA News.

Mr. Mondschein is a member of the Tax Section, Real Property and Probate section, and Elder Law section of the Florida Bar, as well as a member of the Miami-Dade County Probate and Guardianship Committee. He was a speaker on "Planning for ICP Medicaid Qualification with Real Property" at the 3rd Annual Public Benefits Seminar, sponsored by the Elder Law section of the Florida Bar, and was the program chair for the 4th Annual Public Benefits Seminar, as well as the author of "Hospice Medicaid and Qualified Income Trusts" and "Medicaid Recovery, Debunking the Confusion". His article "Beyond the Recovery – a Personal Injury Attorneys Guide to Post Settlement Issues" was published in the Academy of Florida Trial Lawyer's Journal.

Mr. Mondschein has lectured at Certification Review in past years on Long Term Care Insurance, Annuities and Reverse Mortgages. He has lectured on "How to Build an Eldercare Practice" at the Florida Institute of Certified Public Accountants' Multiple-Disciplinary Practice program as well as "Elder Law Update" and "Special Needs Trusts," and at various CPA firms. He spoke at the Florida Bar's annual meeting on "Long Term Care Insurance." He has been named "Chapter Member of the Year" by the Florida Academy of Elder Law Attorneys, and "Member of the Year" by the Elder Law Section of the Florida Bar.

Mr. Mondschein is the featured member in the October/November 2011 issue of The NAELA News. He has been published in the "Daily Business Review" as well as the "South Florida Business Journal" and the Elder Law Newsletter of the Florida Bar's Elder Law section. The firm publishes a monthly newsletter for social workers, discharge planners, nursing home administrators and financial professionals.

Mr. Mondschein is a frequent writer and lecturer on Elder Law and Estate Planning topics. His practice is devoted primarily to Elder Law, Veteran's Benefits, Probate, Guardianship, Estate and Special Needs Planning.

Twyla Sketchley, B.C.S., Attorney

Twyla Sketchley is a Florida Bar Board Certified Elder Law Attorney. She is licensed to practice law in Montana and Florida and founded The Sketchley Law Firm, P.A. in Tallahassee in 2002. She also is Of Counsel to the Bryan Law Firm, P.C. in Bozeman, Montana.

Ms. Sketchley's practice focuses on elder law, guardianship, fiduciary representation, and elder law related litigation. She served as the 2012-2013 Chair of the Elder Law Section of the Florida Bar, 2013-2015 Chair of the Florida Bar's Law Office Management Assistance Service Advisory Board, and the current Chair of the Montana Bar Elder Assistance Committee. In 2016, she founded The Sketchley Method, the nation's leading resource on the prevention of the maltreatment of elders and people with disabilities.

In addition to being an active member of the Florida Bar and its Sections, the National Academy of Elder Law Attorneys, Florida Association for Women Lawyers, and the Montana Bar, Ms. Sketchley is active in her community. She is President of the Academy of Florida Elder Law Attorneys (AFELA), President of the Board of Directors for the North Florida Office of Public Guardian, a board member for FL CHAIN, and a frequent speaker to community organizations regarding elder law issues. She also writes regularly on elder law and practice management issues for statewide publications and has been accepted by Florida courts as an expert in guardianship issues.

Honors & Awards

- 2016 Woman of Distinction in Law Award, Girl Scout Council of the Florida Panhandle
- 2014 Richard W. Ervin Equal Justice Award.
- 2014 National Academy of Elder Law Attorneys Florida Chapter Member of the Year.
- 2011 Florida Association for Women Lawyers Leaders In The Law.
- 2011, 2012, 2013, 2014, 2015, 2016 Florida Super Lawyer.
- 2010, 2011, 2014, 2015, 2016 Florida's Legal Elite.
- 2009, 2010 Florida Super Lawyer Rising Star.
- 2009, 2017 Florida Bar Elder Law Section Charlotte Brayer Award (Public Service).
- 2009 Florida Bar President's Pro Bono Service Award, Second Judicial Circuit.
- 2009 Guardian Angel Award, Office of Public Guardian, Inc.
- Distinguished Woman Award, Smith-Williams Service Center Foundation (October 2008).
- Professionalism Works Award Honoree, The Florida Bar's Henry Latimer Center for Professionalism (July 2008).
- Nominee, Elder Rights Advocacy Hall of Fame, 2008, The National Association of Legal Service Developers.
- Outstanding Legal Services Award, Office of Public Guardian, Inc. (2005).

ENDNOTES

1 John Frazier, Joseph F. Pippen, *Florida Elder Law, Medicaid Planning and Estate Planning*; Rainbow Books, Inc., 2016.

2 "NonLawyer Medicaid Planning Deemed the Unlicensed Practice of Law by Florida Supreme Court," http://estatelegalplanning.com/florida-suprem e-court-medicaid-planning-upl-advisory-opinion/; ("NonLawyer Medicaid Planning") accessed 8/20/17.

3 John Frazier, "Wake up To the Risks Associated with the Use of a NonAttorney for Medicaid Planning," ("Wake Up To the Risks") 2010.

4 Frazier, "Wake up To the Risks."

5 Frazier, "Wake up To the Risks."

6 Frazier, "Wake up To the Risks."

7 Frazier, "Wake up To the Risks."

8 Frazier, "Wake up To the Risks."

9 "NonLawyer Medicaid Planning," http://estatelegalplanning.com/florid a-supreme-court-medicaid-planning-upl-advisory-opinion/.

10 John Frazier, "Durable Power Of Attorney: What You Show Know about UPL (The Unlicensed Practice of Law)," ("Durable Power of Attorney") 2011.

11 "NonLawyer Medicaid Planning," http://estatelegalplanning.com/florid a-supreme-court-medicaid-planning-upl-advisory-opinion/.

12 Frequently Asked Questions About The Florida Bar, Who Can Practice Law In Florida; https://www.floridabar.org/about/faq/#1497453889834-a28b376d-8ccc; accessed 8/20/17.

13 Consumer Pamphlet: Filing an Unlicensed Practice of law Complaint; https://www.floridabar.org/public/consumer/pamphlet012/; ("Consumer Pamphlet") accessed 8/20/17.

14 "Consumer Pamphlet"; https://www.floridabar.org/public/consumer/pamphlet012/; accessed 8/20/17.

15 John Frazier, "The Unlicensed Practice of Law in Medicaid Planning: A Fresh Look at an Old Problem," 2015.

16 "NonLawyer Medicaid Planning," http://estatelegalplanning.com/florid a-supreme-court-medicaid-planning-upl-advisory-opinion/.

17 Florida Statutes Title XLVI Crimes; 777.011 Principal in first degree.— http://www.leg.state.fl.us/Statutes/index.cfm?App_mode=Display_ Statute&URL=0700-0799/0777/0777.html; accessed 8/20/17.

18 John Frazier, *Protecting your Family's Assets: How to Legally Use Medicaid to Pay for Nursing Home and Assisted Living Care*, (Protecting your Family's Assets) 2nd ed. Florida, Rainbow Books Inc., 2012, 176.

19 "NonLawyer Medicaid Planning," http://estatelegalplanning.com/florid a-supreme-court-medicaid-planning-upl advisory-opinion/.

20 John Frazier, "The Cost of Remaining Silent about the Unlicensed Practice of Law," http://estatelegalplanning.com/unlicensed-practice-of-law/; accessed 8/20/17.

21 Consumer Pamphlet: *Filing an Unlicensed Practice of law Complaint*; https:// www.floridabar.org/public/consumer/pamphlet012/; ("Consumer Pamphlet: Filing UPL Complaint") accessed 8/20/17.

22 Florida Bar, "Consumer Pamphlet: Filing UPL Complaint".

23 "Insurance Agents;" http://www.finra.org/investors/insurance-agents; accessed 8/20/17.

24 "Financial Planners," https://www.sec.gov/fast-answers/answersfinplanhtm. html; accessed 8/20/17.

25 "Professional Designations," http://www.finra.org/investors/professional-designations; accessed 8/20/17.

26 Leonard E. Mondschein, "What elder law attorneys need to know about working with non-attorney Medicaid companies" ("What elder law attorneys need to know") *The Elder Law Advocate* Vol. XXII, No. 2 Fall 2015.

27 Mondschein, "What elder law attorneys need to know"

28 "NonLawyer Medicaid Planning," http://estatelegalplanning.com/florid a-supreme-court-medicaid-planning-upl-advisory-opinion/.

29 Frazier, *Protecting your Family's Assets*, 169.

30 Frazier, "Wake up To the Risks."

31 Supreme Court of Florida, SC14-211: The Florida Bar Re: Advisory Opinion – Medicaid Planning Activities by NonLawyers; http://www.floridasupremecourt. org/decisions/2015/sc14-211.pdf; accessed 8/20/17.

32 What is Adult Abuse? Florida Department of Children and Families; http://www.myflfamilies.com/service-programs/adult-protective-services/ what-is-adult-abuse; accessed 8/20/17.

33 Florida Statutes Title XLVI Crimes; Chapter 825 Abuse, Neglect and Exploitation of Elderly Persons and Disabled Adults; http://www.leg.state.fl.us/statutes/index.cfm?App_mode=Display_Statute&URL=0800-0899/0825/0825.html

34 AHCA; If You Have a Concern or Complaint; https://ahca.myflorida.com/MCHQ/Health_Facility_Regulation/Long_Term_Care/docs/Nursing Homes/Posters/NURSING_HOME_POSTER_ENGLISH_LETTER.pdf; accessed 8/20/17.

35 https://www.justice.gov/sites/default/files/elderjustice/legacy/2015/12/15/Florida_Palm_Beaches_LLC.pdf; accessed 8/20/17.

36 Gracey v. Eaker; 837 So.2d 348, 353 (Fla. 2002); http://caselaw.findlaw.com/fl-supreme-court/1218667.html; accessed 8-20-17.

37 https://www.justice.gov/sites/default/files/elderjustice/legacy/2015/12/15/Florida_Palm_Beaches_LLC.pdf; accessed 8/20/17.

38 Ibid.

39 Ibid.

40 Consumer Financial Protection Bureau (CFPB), Protecting residents from financial exploitation, http://files.consumerfinance.gov/f/201406_cfpb_guide_protecting-residents-from-financial-exploitation.pdf; May 2014 ("Protecting Residents"); accessed 8-20-17.

41 http://www.leg.state.fl.us/Statutes/index.cfm?App_mode=Display_Statute&URL=0700-0799/0777/0777.html; Principal in first degree; accessed 8/20/17.

42 "Protecting Residents", http://files.consumerfinance.gov/f/201406_cfpb_guide_protecting-residents-from-financial-exploitation.pdf.

43 42 U.S. Code § 1320b–25 - Reporting to law enforcement of crimes occurring in federally funded long-term care facilities; https://www.law.cornell.edu/uscode/text/42/1320b-25; accessed 9/5/17.

44 Florida Statutes Title XXIX Public Health; Nursing Homes and Related Health Care Facilities; 400.17 Bribes, kickbacks, certain solicitations prohibited. http://www.leg.state.fl.us/Statutes/index.cfm?App_mode=Display_Statute&Search_String=&URL=0400-0499/0400/Sections/0400.17.html

45 Frazier, "Wake up To the Risks."

46 NAELA News, Oct-Nov-Dec 2016, "The History of the Florida Medicaid Planning UPL Advisory Opinion," John Frazier, http://estatelegalplanning.com/wp-content/uploads/NAELA-News-Frazier-Article.pdf; accessed 8/20/17.

47 Frazier, "Wake up To the Risks."